The
RevPAR
FORMULA

OCC + ADR = RevPAR

The RevPAR FORMULA

Optimizing **C**hallenging **C**ircumstances plus
Always **D**riving **R**etention
equals an increase in
Revenue **P**er **A**vailable **R**oom.

Jokima Hiller & Jill Woods

Outskirts Press, Inc.
Denver, Colorado

The RevPAR Formula
OCC + ADR = RevPAR

Outskirts Press, Inc.
http://www.outskirtspress.com

ISBN: 978-1-4327-7051-8

PRINTED IN THE UNITED STATES OF AMERICA

This guide is for every overworked and frustrated manager, shift supervisor, and star employee who's ever worked in the hospitality industry and wondered "What the hell did I get myself into?" There is indeed a "light at the end of the tunnel" and it is called OCC+ADR=RevPAR! **O**ptimizing **C**hallenging **C**ircumstances plus **A**lways **D**riving **R**etention leads to an increase in your property's **Rev**enue **P**er **A**vailable **R**oom.

In an industry where you work with people every day, challenging circumstances are bound to happen. . .a desk clerk calls off or a sales manager gets discouraged. But, by focusing on our formula you will be empowered to optimize these circumstances thereby lessening time wasted, yielding stronger, more engaged employees who will take care of the guest. It is this employee and guest interaction that will lead to sustainable profits.

In this easy to read quick reference guide, we will address ten common circumstances that you will have, or have had in your hospitality career. Resolutions, suggestions, and advice are offered along with our true to life background stories detailing our journey in the hotel business. Whether you take it or leave it, undeniably you'll be able to relate, cry, and probably do much more laughing as you read this book and continue on your own path!

Contents

———⦿———

What Has Been Your Most Challenging Circumstance in Your Hospitality Career?

Anonymous Industry Professional

I see the biggest daily challenge is to help hotels complete long term strategic planning. The challenge of managing day to day operations makes many GM's and Managers very reactive and short sighted, while long term strategy and planning gets ignored to put out the more immediate fires. This creates future issues which could have been avoided by more long term planning.

I guess basically, the challenge is being able to have your "hands" in so many areas and providing excellent internal and external customer service through example and communication.

Terri Caldwell, General Manager

I come in to work with a list of definite "to do's". Not a very big list, but "must be done's". At the end of the day, my list is partially done, I leave for home late. Then head back for more of the same the next day.

Gwen Hasse, Hospitality & Restaurant Management Program Instructor

After working in restaurant operations for 20 + years and now teaching people to go into the industry, I have been able to see my challenges with the industry.

Daily the challenge is keeping your employees motivated to provide excellent customer service. In turn, finding the time daily to provide the training for your staff to understand what excellent service is. So many factors play into being able to provide excellent customer service and juggling them while being profitable and providing an excellent work environment for your internal guests. For example, as a manager you must be able to meet your labor cost goals while making sure that the internal customers make money and your external customers are delighted.

Cecelia Jernegan, Director of Sales

The difficult part of working at a hotel is between 7am and 5pm when the majority of time is spent taking care of the guests and developing the staff. The detailed paper work, e-mails and correspondence must be completed during the evenings or on the weekends. Managers at the hotel level need to make their staff, ownership, brand and guests all happy. The 2 sentences above causes "burn out" for managers. The turnover rate for hotel managers within 2 years is around 70%. The pay is low and generally no benefits. However, for some the hotel industry is NOT a job but a way of life. If one knows how to balance work/life the hotel industry can be fun and fulfilling. The job is making good memories for the guest that visit our home away from their home whether for business or play.

Shelly Legas Leydecker, General Manager
My biggest struggle is...

Every time I am fully in a train of thought, I seem to get interrupted by an employee. I feel that my open door policy creates a lot of mismanaged time. I feel too guilty telling my housekeepers/ desk staff/ or maint. employees that I don't have time to discuss their issue right now...so I stop what I am doing and listen to them. Then I have to get myself back into the mode of doing the interrupted task. This is VERY challenging for me. The GM has sooooooo many balls to juggle daily...but other employees don't realize that requesting a time would be much more helpful... and I would be more focused on their issue rather than worried I will forget where I was!

Michael Pearson, Night Auditor
The greatest aspect of the hotel business is that it is never boring and you can absolutely count on each day bringing a fresh batch of challenges that will test you. That said, management of your own attitude determines your own success or failure in handling these challenges properly.

With employees, you must demonstrate patience and understanding when it comes to training and counseling; with guest issues, especially when you are being yelled at, you must be empathetic yet firm. And almost without fail, if you have a day that doesn't present you with employee and guest issues, you can count on the property itself testing your fortitude and patience.

David Rains, Front Office Manager

My biggest daily challenge would have to be ensuring that the hotel is living up to the expectations put forth by not only our guests, but by our owners as well. Sometimes what's best for one is not always in the best interest for the other. This is particularly true concerning rates and other costs; you want to make sure you're consistently a good value to the guest, but you also have business objectives to consider.

David Todd Reynolds, Supervisor

The biggest challenge any hotel faces is the human factor. Keeping employees and front line workers happy and motivated, trained and informed, and meeting their needs and desires is a daily exercise that you have to be committed to and practice at in order to be successful.

Anthony Turner, General Manager

Speaking from the perspective of a manager that is still

"ramping up" a new property, I'd say balancing the critical art of helping my staff understand that customer service at its core is the most important job in the world. But it does not mean that we are not in business to make money. While keeping the staff engaged with the customer it is important to keep in mind that we can not give away the store.

Ryan White, Vice President of Operations
I think the biggest challenges that manager's face is not only managing their people but also figuring out how to engage, motivate and build trusted relationships with their employees. Manager's that are able to connect with each of their employees and create a strong team have overall better results than those that struggle to connect with their teams. My motto has always been and still is today, "I won't ask you to do something that I haven't done or something that I'm not willing to do myself."

Challenging Circumstance # 1
Attendance

When there are major attendance issues in regards to employees, a business, especially one in the hospitality industry, tends to die a slow and painful death. We sell experiences in our hotels, restaurants, cafes, shops, clubs, casinos and when everybody's late or someone fails to show, guest experiences become negatively impacted. What kind of experience did we sell that day when Donny missed pre-shift at 8:00am and Tracy called-off? Keep in mind this may have just been ONE department! What if similar circumstances were happening in the housekeeping, maintenance, and sales areas simultaneously?

A manager of a business walks a fine line each day, trying to be sensitive to an employees' life outside of work while trying to keep the business profitable so the employee still has a job to go to. This is a challenge all businesses are facing especially in these economic times. What sounds like a nightmare day and evening for one manager who covers for tardy and absent associates is actually the sign of a much larger problem. What if that manager had appointments scheduled that day that could have greatly impacted the hotels success and job stability for all involved? What if other employees were stepping in to fill the gap accumulating costly overtime?

Each employee makes a daily choice to positively or negatively affect others on their job. Here's what you can do to optimize this top industry challenge:

- Ensure Employees are in the Right Position

- Share the Businesses Financial Results

- Review your Attendance Policy

- Hold Associates Accountable

If people are in positions where they can't function to their full potential, they are most likely to miss work. Maybe they weren't properly trained or simply aren't good at their job. Not everyone can multi-task which is a key skill for a hotel front desk clerk. Or, maybe the new restaurant server does poorly because they can't remember the daily specials. Seek to place employees in positions where they can thrive and contribute their very best.

Sometimes associates don't understand the effects and impact chronic absenteeism and tardiness has on a department and organization. Share the companies financial results on a regular basis and then illustrate how much more money could have been made or how much money the business lost due to attendance issues. Be sure to address overtime, possibility of guest complaints, and daily responsibilities gone unassigned.

It is possible that the attendance policy itself is confusing or perhaps unreasonable. Policies that are punitive set employees up for failure. Review your current policy and ensure that it is clear and offers associates a guideline for success.

Holding associates accountable is one of the biggest challenges for a manager. No one wants to be the bad guy. If you're the boss, it is highly likely you're going to be considered the bad guy anyway! Being lax in enforcing policies won't change what the team thinks of you; in fact, by not holding associates accountable, you'll lose the respect of those who are being accountable. If someone has abused the policy it is imperative that they receive the consequences as indicated. This will impress upon other associates the importance of this necessary policy.

Author Notes: *It was approximately 1:00am in the morning as I sat in my office hovered over a garbage can with one eye on the camera that was focused on the hotel's front desk. I was sick and it had been at least a decade since the last time I had vomited. Yet I, General Manager of a hotel with a full and capable staff was stuck working at a time when I felt my worse. Why? Let's look at the events of the day . . .*

Donny, who was the night auditor, was late. His shift started 2 hours ago and he insisted that he was "on his way!" But, the damage was already done – my bed, medicine, and easy background music would have to wait.

Donny had no idea of the impact his tardiness had on the rest of the team, our financial status, and me, his general manager. So, I showed him along with the rest of the staff in our next all team meeting. - Jokima

Challenging Circumstance # 2
Uniforms

Getting employees to wear their uniform seems to be a problem across many disciplines. . .from department stores and gas stations to restaurants and hotels. As a customer, it is hard to ask for assistance because you cannot identify who are employees of the organization. A uniformed staff sets the image of the business, gives guests confidence in knowing who to go to in case of an emergency or if help is needed, and instills pride in associates. In addition, some uniforms are designed for protection according to the employees role and responsibilities. Therefore, they are important and should be worn in a clean and professional manner.

1. Many times in the hospitality industry it is found that employees spend more time at work than they do at home! Therefore, what they wear everyday to work should be a uniform that is not demeaning yet one that they could be proud to wear. More and more today, hospitality uniforms are looking more like your everyday business attire.

Employees do not have to be in something that makes every guest point and say, "Look, there's an employee!" But, company-logo'd uniform apparel and nametags would suffice in identifying employees. Uniforms should be modern and relevant.

2. Supervisors and managers should be willing to set the example. This may be a tough one; but, if employees see the boss wearing their uniform believing that it is good enough for the "big cheese" makes it good enough for them. Consider changing up colors or adding a high quality nametag for supervisors so that they can be identified as so.

3. Treat being provided uniforms by the company as a benefit. Make sure it is listed on the benefits page of new hire paperwork and employee handbooks. Talk it up right along with health insurance and/ or paid holidays. Many times employees can see quicker the money saved in wear and tear of their own clothes; but, you may need to bring this to their attention. Also, it is a benefit to not have to agonize over what you're wearing today! The decision is made for you and it makes getting ready for work stress free.

4. Who gets fired for not wearing the proper footwear? It sounds very petty; but, what if something fell on that persons foot while at work? Wearing the proper uniform must be an employee responsibility that is enforced on a daily basis and yes, management must be willing to terminate an associate for chronic violations of this requirement.

Set the expectation in the beginning that uniforming is important, refer to it as an employee benefit, make sure the selected uniforms are professional, get managers involved, and then be willing to enforce the rules.

Author Notes: I remember when I took over as front desk manager at a full-service hotel. Other department heads would say to me "good luck" and "may the force be with you!" I knew I was up for a challenge and was frankly terrified of the infamous trouble making staff I was about to supervise!

I realized that no one, especially the ladies, were wearing the appropriate uniform. I had to change our environment and quickly. I ordered a front desk uniform for myself, threw on a pair of heels, and added some cute earrings and a big smile! The very first day I stepped behind the front desk my new staff commented how "sharp" I looked. I told them to look in the mirror and much to their surprise they realized that I was wearing the SAME EXACT uniform! - Jokima

Challenging Circumstance # 3
Handling Guest Complaints

A t times the most difficult thing for a hotel employee or manager is to hear criticism - whether it
is about the job they are doing, their hotel or their co-
workers or employee. After all, we are trained to have a
deep sense of pride about our hotel and the job we do.
So - how do you handle a verbal attack in the form of a
guest complaint.

As a guide in the service industry, if you have been
working in a hotel for any length of time - you have
observed situations where a guest is irritated about
something. Maybe they found something in their room
that should not be there, or their reservation was not
accurate. You have also likely watched as a front desk
agent or manager struggled to listen to the guest or come
up with a solution that pleases the guest and the hotel.
The hotel business runs on the ability to attract repeat
customers; they are the bread and butter by which we
pay the bills and the employees of the hotel.

How do you stay calm in the face of a very upset guest?

Your step by step process for handling complaints well: - If the guest is at the front desk around other guests, try to take them aside to a quieter area if possible.

- Take a deep breath, and listen - looking into their face and nod to acknowledge that you hear them.

- When they stop talking, ask a couple of questions to make sure you understand the situation properly. This also shows them that you were listening. This could be all they wanted in the first place.

- Once you understand the situation, apologize. You can simply say "I am so sorry that happened and I understand your frustration." Think about it - once the apology is out there - there is no debate on the issue. The guest can relax and feel heard.

- Ask the guest, what can we do to make this better? Yes, you may have a guest or two that will ask for the moon - but more often than not, the guest will be so impressed by your attention and apology - that a small discount or upgrade will please them.

- Follow up to make sure whatever you offered them happens. This also gives you the opportunity to contact the guest and show how important they are to your business.

Author Notes: *I was managing a hotel that was sold out for the weekend with a ... cheerleading competition. I will admit, not having been a cheerleader in my younger days, that I could not understand the purpose of a competition involving the sport of cheerleading. I was already in a mood to want to avoid any guest complaints and that is like waiving a red flag in front of a bull. For there will never be enough clean towels, hot water for showers and patience for this group.*

Of course, one of our hot water heaters malfunctioned on the first morning of this competition, meaning a few rooms ran out of hot water early. Our maintenance staff acted quickly and by mid-morning, all hot water heaters were back in service. But not in enough time to avoid a cold shower for one man and his three daughters. He proceeded to call the hotel, asking to talk to the GM - throughout the entire day and insisting that the front desk staff comp their room for the whole weekend. Wanting to avoid giving a refund for a situation beyond our control and that we had fixed so quickly, I avoided responding to his call, until it was time for me to go home that day. I thought - if he came back to the hotel and had hot water - his anger would be gone and we could simply discount his room. I was mistaken... - Jill

Challenging Circumstance # 4
Department Wars

Yes, employees in the hospitality industry sometimes don't get along! Many times this is because they are so passionate about their roles, department, and contribution to the organization that they believe that no one else could possibly be working as hard. So, front-of-the-house associates get mad at back-of-the-house associates, housekeepers blame front desk clerks, and no one likes the sales department! Yet, it is the internal guest that can make or break an external guest's experience. Therefore, we must work together as a team and not be at war.

Establish Value Relative to Responsibilities
Salaries in most businesses are a taboo subject. But, guess what? Mostly every employee is talking about it and possibly embellishing the amount of their compensation. So, why not minimize this chatter by posting starting pay per department in employment ads, pre-employment paperwork, or in the breakroom for all to see? Reality is that our pay/salary is tied to our value in an organization. What this means is that the more you make, the more work you

do. For example, if housekeepers see that their work is valued the same as front desk clerks, this will most often prevent a war.

Understand the Job Description

"They don't even do anything in the sales department but sit and answer the phone!" Does this sound familiar? Clearly, the person making this comment is unaware of the responsibilities and activities that go in the sales area. So, tell them. Consider having a "show and tell" at staff meetings allowing each department an opportunity to be in the spotlight. Employees can share their job descriptions, their department's key objectives, and show some of the work and challenges they encounter throughout their week. Understanding what a night auditor does when no one else is there to see what they do is crucial to preventing a war.

Cross Train

Sometimes people need more than a show and tell, they need to do! What's the saying? - "Experience is the best teacher!" In a time when guests want their requests filled in a timely manner and their issues resolved on the spot; you don't want to risk having one person on staff saying "I can't help you." Requiring employees to learn and practice one more area other than the one they are assigned helps them better understand the challenges of their co-workers but also puts them in a position to better serve the guest.

Author Notes: *I knew that if I didn't do something soon that I'd be attending someone's funeral and we'd be on the front page of the newspaper! The newspaper headline would have read, "Front Desk Staff Checks Each Other in BUT They Don't Check Out!" The day shift was feuding with the evening shift, the evening shift was feuding with the night audit shift, and the night audit shift was feuding with the day shift. It was a mess!*

At our next front desk meeting, I had representatives from each shift role play activities that happened on a daily basis. They shared their shift checklists and talked about what they needed from other shifts to make their jobs a bit easier. I announced that they would also cross train and learn each shift by rotating and working two weeks on each shift. Although, this was not received well, when the rotations concluded everyone admitted that they truly had no clue how difficult it was to work the other shifts! Now, they understood.

Finally, I created a form that applicants of the front office area received when completing an application. The form listed some standard information about the hotel, benefits offered to full-time and part-time associates, and the starting pay for each line level position. This set the expectation from day one that if you're hired as the night auditor making a bit more than other shifts, more would be expected of you in that role. Your pay was relative to your responsibilities. - Jokima

Challenging Circumstance # 5
Time Management

T ime Management is always a sensitive topic for hotel managers and employees. As a manager, you want to convey a calm competent exterior at all times - but anyone in this business knows you have half a million to-do-lists racing through your mind. There is a fine line between delegating tasks to appropriate employees so you are not overwhelmed, and being seen as a manager who is simply a figure head but does mostly nothing towards running their hotel. Being too efficient with your time can make you appear curt and detached from the warm, welcoming feeling the hospitality business is all about. If you have ever watched TV shows like *Hotel* or *Hotel Babylon*, you get to see the frantic scrambling behind the scenes to make deadlines, and the relaxed expression which is clearly faked on the face of the hotel manager.

You can attend all the time management classes or read the books, but putting those ideas into action seems like it has to change your entire life. Try one of these ideas for a week or two - and see what works for you:

- Is there one daily or weekly task that you dread? Find a partner and schedule this as one of the first things to tackle each day - leaving these tasks towards the end of the day or week just builds into the anxiety you already feel towards this item.

- Is there a task that you could use as a training exercise for one of the staff members you are trying to develop into management? Use your time doing this to train someone else on it, you just may find this will benefit you and engage this employee at the same time.

- **Never delay sales or networking tasks for paperwork.** Owners and management companies usually understand delayed reports; but, putting off sales activities are like delaying revenue and no one wants that.

- Keep up on short term and long term goals by having action plans for each week.

- Make really large projects smaller by devoting 20 minutes per day into them. You are more likely to not only meet deadlines, but end up finishing large projects ahead of time.

- If you are overwhelmed, don't be afraid to admit it to someone you can trust. Sometimes talking through your list out loud with someone else clears your mind and makes it easier to tackle the hard stuff.

Author Notes: I remember participating in the pre-opening activities of a hotel. As general manager, I was responsible for a myriad of tasks including hiring staff and setting up vendor accounts. I operated in what I called "organized chaos." I probably still function that way today! My cell phone bill was more than I care to admit to in writing! I realized in the midst of this process, that I needed help.

Let me be honest, help was there, I felt I just couldn't use it. After all, if you want something done right. . .you know how that saying goes. I began to think about why I couldn't delegate and it was because I wasn't sure that my newly hired team could 1) Do the task that I'd be asking or 2) Perform the task to my level of expectation. "But, couldn't I teach them?" I thought. Yes, I could and so I did. I took the overtime I was putting in trying to handle everything and sat down one-on-one with my staff and trained them on the activities that needed to be accomplished. This freed me up to tackle other responsibilities or to at least make it home in time for dinner.

The truly rewarding thing about learning to manage my time through delegation was that I was planting the seeds for my staff to be independent. After investing the time with them in the beginning to take care of the business of the hotel, they became confident that they could do the work and I was able to trust that they could deliver. - Jokima

Challenging Circumstance # 6
Employee Engagement

What is Employee Engagement? An "engaged employee" is one who is fully participative in the workplace, bringing both their heart and head to their role. Simply put - they care.

Why do you want an engaged employee on your team? Ideally, you want every employee to be engaged. Look at how they make a difference:

- **Non-Engaged Employee on Board** - Walks by trash sitting in the hallway of the business.

- **Engaged Employee on Board** - Stops, picks up, and discards trash in the hallway.

- **Non-Engaged Employee on Board** – Works late; but, complains or looks for a reward.

- **Engaged Employee on Board** – Works late willingly without complaint.

- **Non-Engaged Employee on Board** – Creates problems and turmoil.

- **Engaged Employee on Board** – Offers resolutions.

- **Non-Engaged Employee on Board** – Stuck in their ways even when presented with a better way.

- **Engaged Employee on Board** – Always willing to learn and grow.

How do you work towards having an engaged staff? First, make sure you're not trying to convert "warm bodies." It is highly likely your efforts will not bring forth the results that you seek. Next, keeping your team engaged is an on-going process. As you review the suggestions below, consider employing one, a few, or all, keeping in mind your budget:

- **Get to Know Your Staff** – Find out what recognition means to them and how they prefer to be recognized. You need to know what motivates and drives them – is it family, a better life, money, title, etc. Likewise, you'll need to share a bit about yourself. Transparency helps you build trust with your team.

- **Develop Individuals** – Prepare developmental plans for each team member. The developmental plan can consist of professional and/or personal goals. The purpose is to "invest" in the individual employee. Hospitality employees may spend more time at work than at home. Therefore, it is imperative that the place that they're devoted to returns the loyalty by taking stock in their progress.

- **Make Employees Experts** – Everyone wants to feel needed and have a sense of belongingness. What better way to facilitate this by training associates so that they master specific areas of their position? Yes, they must be able to perform all of the tasks their role requires; but, to be proficient and an expert at one task sets them up to be asked questions, consulted when problems arise and a resolution is needed, and allows them to always be on the look out for improvements. Take this a step further and assign titles according to their chief talent. Order nametags or business cards with these titles. . .having troubles with the point-of-sale printer? Call The POS Peacekeeper!

- **Recognize To Reinforce** – Recognition is necessary and key to the engagement process. It needs to be frequent, documented, constant, timely, informal & formal, warranted, and personalized. Recognition can be a pat on the back, a handwritten note or a pin, plaque, or day off with pay. How do you know what works for your team? You should gather this info as you get to know them. Most importantly, the fact that recognition takes place at your organization should be publicized and talked about often and in high regard. This will reinforce the positive behavior and actions of the engaged leaving the unengaged wondering how they can participate.

- **Keep Everyone Informed** – "How do I contribute to our company goals?" An engaged employee will want this question answered for them. They need to know that they are making a difference. Hold staff meetings and discuss the business's mission, objectives, customer comments, financial results, failures, and successes. Offer details on how each associate supports these results.

Most importantly, make sure employees have all of the necessary tools, materials, and training they need to do their jobs well!

Author Notes: I came in really early one morning and noticed we had bananas as a part of our breakfast offering.

This caught me by surprise because bananas weren't an item we ordered through our foodservice provider. In fact, it was a great debate in our company on whether or not we should provide this fruit. So, where did they come from?

I asked my night auditor, Monica, who's responsible for setting up the breakfast if she knew how we got bananas. She said "I buy them and put them out every morning that I know our railroad guys will be staying with us. They're up so early and they like bananas because it's something easy they can tuck in their pocket as they head off to work. It makes them soo happy!" As I processed what Monica had said, I asked her who was paying for these bananas. Her response changed my life – it validated my efforts in maintaining an engaged team. Monica said "Ms. Jokima you stay up late some nights just to bring me two double cheeseburgers from Burger King only because you know that I like them! If you can do that for me, I can do the same for our guests."

Monica was one of the best night auditors I ever had and I owe it all to double cheeseburgers! - Jokima

Challenging Circumstance # 7
Preventing Burnout

The hotel industry is a pretty fast-paced and demanding business in which there will inevitably be a time when both employees and managers may feel that tiny amounts of their very being, intelligence if you will, is being chipped away by serving others. When you give of yourself physically, mentally, and emotionally sometimes you lose YOUR sharpness, intensity, and/or effectiveness. Many times this is what adults characterize as "burn-out." It happens to even the best of us! A sure-fire way to prevent this psychological experience of exhaustion and diminished interest is to practice honing on a regular basis.

Between the many uses and occasional sharpening of a knife, it may need to be honed. To "hone," according to the *Merriam-Webster Dictionary*, means to make more acute, intense, or effective. You see, a knife's cutting edge becomes reshaped over time from sharpening. Tiny amounts of the blade are being ground away as Chef Danilo Alfaro explains.

How can you continue to sharpen others when you, yourself have lost some of your sharpness?

Honing can happen in a variety of ways:

- Read a book that inspires you and strengthens your passion for what you do!

- Take a class or go back to school!

- Join a club or networking organization!

- Hear a powerful guest speaker!

- Go on a field trip and take a tour of some place that ignites a spark of enthusiasm!

- Watch an inspiring movie!

- Conduct your own research on the internet!

- Try cooking a new dish, clean a guestroom, or reconnect with whatever drew you to your profession in the first place!

The key is to learn and enhance or refresh your skill set! Do this on a regular basis. If you're a Chef, join the

American Culinary Federation. If you're a recent hospitality graduate, start building your library of industry magazines or books. If you're a maintenance employee, take a class created just for you that's offered by the Educational Institute of America. If you are in a role specifically designed to sharpen (teach, train, share your knowledge and who you are) others, then this one's for you – "Honing on a regular basis, keeps the burn-out away!"

Author Notes: Jill was on her seventh day straight of working more than 10 hour days. We'd just hired several new employees and getting them trained was her mission. Current employees had already started in on these "newbies" telling them tales of how management was mean. I believe it was at this point that Jill had allowed the trials of this industry get to her. She could no longer resist feeling discouraged or that her efforts were in vain. She was second-guessing her every move, our goals and wondered if we'd make it to that "light at the end of the tunnel". Her mood and concentration was altered. She was burned out! It was just a matter of time before she slipped up or made such a blunder as showing up with one brown shoe on her right foot and one black shoe on her left foot.

What makes Jill's mishap so troubling is that we had attended a networking event that morning. There were a great number of people in attendance and not one person mentioned her shoes! We assumed that the seemingly extra attention we were getting that morning was just because we were attractive and interesting hotel managers. We can laugh now! - Jokima

Challenging Circumstance #8
Sales Slump

There is nothing more discouraging than having your normally peppy and positive Sales Manager lose their "fire" for their job and the hotel business. This can be the result of so many factors:

- Hearing too many "no's" in one week. Rejection from potential clients is a big downer.

- Increased pressure from owners/management to produce during an already challenging economy.

- Accounts not being taken care of properly by other staff at the hotel. A Sales Manager needs to know that the account they have "won over" will be taken care of by the rest of the hotel staff.

- A lack of support and training - from their supervisor, brand or management company.

- Personal life issues are following them to work - sucking their energy and focus from the task at hand.

- A lack of fun! Yes, it is true - a Sales Representative has to feel their job is fun and entertaining. After all - they are representing a product that they should not only like but feel proud of.

A Sales Manager has to be "on" all the time - always ready to be the example of hospitality for the hotel.

What can be done? If you are their supervisor, look for ways to guide them into re-discovering their passion for their job:

- Remind them of a past success where they won an account and how proud the staff and management was of them.

- Attend a sales call with them, let them lead the call and be encouraging of their skills and relationship with clients.

- Ask them what they feel is missing from their job - and how you can help.

Are you the one in the sales slump?

- Re-charge your batteries by attending a sales seminar, or listening to an inspirational speaker or music on your way to work.

- Had a bad sales call? Always know a few clients that are happy to see you, and visit one next. The sooner you get back on the horse, the better for your confidence.

- Go to lunch with your favorite mentor, share stories and laugh. Remember how much fun this can be, after all you are not stuck in the hotel - you have the freedom to get out and be in the community.

Author Notes: The last three offices I had visited, had pointed to the "no soliciting" sign like I was there bothering them to buy my goods. I only wanted to drop off some cookies and information about my hotel in case they had visitors in need of accommodations.

Cold calls are never easy, but it had just started to rain and I was losing my positive outlook for my job today. Just up ahead was the office of one of my favorite clients, the Administrative Assistant Donna. She loved it when

I would stop in with cookies and usually had some good information about upcoming events for the company.

Twenty minutes later, I was ready to tackle that last cold call. Donna had been thrilled to see me, as she had a meeting room and block of rooms to book with me! - Jill

Challenging Circumstance # 9
Warm Body Syndrome

Human Resources can be a dirty word in the hotel business. . .ask any hiring manager. Some of the lowest paying jobs in this industry involve the most interaction with the guests. Think about that for a minute or two – each guest interacts with your lowest paid employees more than anyone else. Whether you are in limited service, select, or full service, this is a reality check like no other. After all – not everyone wants to or will have the skill set and desire to be in management, so what is their motivation to provide the best performance each day? This question should be a part of the interview as there are many warm bodies in this industry, taking up space to earn a paycheck with nothing more to offer. At some point – you may ask yourself, "Don't we have to have workers like that?" Most hotels do have those folks and it is called planned turnover – they don't often get promotions or raises and they eventually move on to the next place for 25 cents an hour more. Realistically, it happens and we all know it.

As long as those employees are not costing us in other areas, it is okay to have a few of those on board. Or is it?

Taking in a warm body employee, who is not motivated to acquire more knowledge and grow in their career – can often taint the rest of the staff. It is a slow moving poison that you don't feel until it is about to kill you and then it is too late to suck out the poison. Once they are there, it is hard to get them out. Maybe they never do enough bad stuff to get fired, and yet, not enough good stuff to remain on the team you are building. If you've ever wondered if "one bad apple could spoil the bunch" just try hiring an unengaged employee. Never forget it is a team you are building, and sometimes being the coach is making those tough calls on who needs to be benched.

The resolution to this common industry ailment is really tough. But, if you truly want to run or work for a business that is optimizing challenging circumstances and driving retention, leading to a healthy and sustainable RevPAR, then listen carefully. . .don't do it! Trust us, you don't need that employee to work for you if even for just a day. One day turns into a week and then you're looking at how did things get so out of control. The best way to prevent having unengaged employees is not hire warm bodies to begin with. Now this may mean you pull additional shifts, work night audit, take work home, miss a planned vacation, or lunch with grandma; but, hold out for that rock star you deserve to have on your team.

If you find that you have hired an unengaged employee or you've taken over a department or company that has this type of associate then show them as little attention as possible. This employee will dry up like a fruit and will go away. Shower your staff that IS giving their best with all of your time and attention. The warm body will wonder why the tables have turned and no one is complaining about them or asking them "what's wrong?" and "what can I do to help you do a better job?"

Author Notes: I guess I am to blame for this situation. . .I asked Jill to join me in managing a hotel that was running rampant with warm bodies! Regardless of the hotel's occupancy, two front desk clerks were on duty at all times in addition to a driver. There were days when the staff would pile into the hotel's van leaving one associate at the desk and they'd go to the grocery store! And, everyone was just fine with being paid for an 8-hour work day without working. They'd sit around in the back office and chat about their spouses or what was for lunch. As I tried to tighten up the schedule taking into consideration customer demand, life got so difficult. As Jill and I would bring on willing workers, the existing crew would fill them with stories of how things used to be. . .trips to the store, time to sit around and chat and then we'd have another unengaged associate on our hands.

As General Manager I clocked more hours than I had starting out as a young, naïve manager. As these fruits dried up one by one by our lack of interest we began to see that "light at the end of the tunnel". Did we make it Jill? We made it and we lived to write about it! - Jokima

Challenging Circumstance #10
Cleaning House

C leaning house has such a negative connation. And, in most situations it really should be a last resort, after all the staff that is in place was put there for some reason.

There are several cases where "cleaning house" or a total staff turnover can happen:

1. Unless you work for a hotel with one owner who also manages the business and will the rest of your life - it is likely you will be in a situation where you have to answer to several bosses. This can be challenging in normal circumstances, but in a tumultuous economy it can mean having a new management company come in and take over the hotel. Often this means the new management company has the option of hiring an all new staff.

2. A new Manager is hired, and brings many changes that the current staff is unable or not willing to make.

3. Guest Complaints are on the rise, and all departments at the hotel are under scrutiny. Owners or Upper Management may choose to have a job fair and replace most or all employees.

New Management Company = New Everything. Will you be replaced by someone "newer"? How do you survive and do you want to?

- Are you a part of the problem or the solution? There are often two kinds of employees, those that always come to you with issues, and those that are "fixers". Fixers choose to focus on helping or resolving issues and are seen as great examples of teamwork.

- Can you adjust your thinking and learn new processes? Or do you have a routine and hate the thought of adjusting or adding to your workload? When a new manager or management company comes on-site, they are observing to see which employees are open to change and which ones argue that "this is the way we have always done it".

- Always be a student! Be ready to learn something from anyone who has something to offer - maybe it is a "what not to do" lesson. Either way, be open to change and the knowledge that comes from those situations that test you. It is all learning, and when we cease to learn - we stop living.

Author Notes: *Jokima was back and thrilled to be managing a hotel again. Her enthusiasm for the hotel business and training employees was overflowing. There were so many incentive ideas she had, and she was sure the staff would be thrilled at how they could earn more money.*

Until the first week...

No one wanted her there. They loved the last GM and how he let them run the hotel, they could do whatever they wanted and it was fun. Who did she think she was? She was crushed, and no one - including the assistant manager and sales manager - was on her team. They looked for ways to discourage and discredit her. She needed a partner, at least one person who would be on her team – ME! It was becoming obvious that the current staff would have to go. This was a much larger job than she was led to believe... - Jill

About the Authors

Jill Woods has served the hospitality industry for over 20 years, and values the lessons that The Frosty Mug, The Olive Garden, Ruby Tuesdays, Hampton Inns and Country Inns & Suites have taught her about serving others.

She's held many coveted industry roles including Director of Sales, Assistant General Manager, and General Manager. Having experienced many challenging circumstances, Jill has implemented and perfected ideas in the areas of networking, event planning, training, and human resource development and tracking.

In her rare off time, she enjoys reading, traveling and spending time with her husband Kevin, daughter Jourdan and family dog Sophia.

She aspires to own and operate a training hotel where employees are prepared to take on leadership positions in the hospitality industry.

Follow Jill on Twitter @jillwhotelsales

Jokima Hiller's passion to please has helped her sustain an amazing career in the hospitality industry since the age of 15 and her blend of experience and education make her a great resource for students.

Jokima has held a variety of positions ranging from Human Resources Clerk and Assistant Reservation Sales Manager to Front Office Manager and General Manager. Her ability to take what she's learned on the job and in the classroom and share it with others made her an ideal trainer for the Radisson Hotel and Country Inns & Suites By Carlson hotel brands. Her Bachelor degree in Restaurant, Hotel, Institutional, & Tourism Management and Masters in Business Administration put her in positions to actually create, not just follow, best practices adopted by hotel colleagues, management and franchise companies. She has thoroughly enjoyed impacting the lives of hotel owners, managers, employees, and guests and is looking forward to having that same positive impact on students as well.

Her life's goal is to be the best aunt in the world. It is through her passion for hotels that she plans to own her own hotel providing an opportunity to build Auntie Jody's House, a home away from home for foster children.

Follow Jokima on Twitter @JLHiller